ROSE

Rose

Rose is a survivor. Her remarkable life began
in a tiny Russian village, took her to Warsaw's
ghettos and a ship called *The Exodus* and
finally to the boardwalks of Atlantic City, the
Arizona Canyons and salsa-flavoured nights in
Miami Beach.

The play is a portrait of a feisty Jewish
woman and a reminder of some of the events
that shaped the twentieth century.

Martin Sherman

ROSE

Methuen

First published in the United Kingdom in 1999 by
Methuen Publishing Limited
215 Vauxhall Bridge Road, London, SW1V 1EJ

Peribo Pty Ltd, 58 Beaumont Road, Mount Kuring-Gai,
NSW 2080, Australia, ACN 002 273 761
(for Australia and New Zealand)

ISBN 0-7394-1076-8

Typeset by SX Composing DTP, Rayleigh, Essex
Printed and bound in Great Britain
by Cox & Wyman Ltd, Reading, Berkshire

For Elizabeth Shapiro

Martin Sherman was born in Philadelphia and educated at Boston University. His plays include: *Bent* (Royal Court Theatre, London, 1979; subsequently, West End and Broadway); *Messiah* (Hampstead Theatre, London, 1983); *What She Danced* (Guildford/King's Head Theatre, London, 1988); *A Madhouse in Goa* (Lyric Hammersmith, London, 1989); *Some Sunny Day* (Hampstead Theatre, 1996). Films include: *Clothes in the Wardrobe* (BBC Television, 1992; subsequent cinema release in the US under the title of *The Summer House*, 1994); *Alive and Kicking* (1997); *Bent* (1998). He has lived in London since 1980.

Rose was first performed in the Cottesloe auditorium at the Royal National Theatre on 19 May 1999. The cast was as follows:

Rose Olympia Dukakis

Directed by Nancy Meckler
Designed by Stephen Brimson Lewis
Lighting by Johanna Town

ROSE

Rose *sits on a wooden bench. She is eighty. There is a bottle of water and a glass on the bench, as well as a refridgerated pack. Occasional noise can be heard outside.*

Rose   She laughed. And then she blew her nose. She had a cold. The bullet struck her forehead. It caught her in the middle of a thought. She was nine.

Pause.

I'm sitting shivah. You sit shivah for the dead.

Pause.

Shivah sounds like the name of a Hindu god. Maybe it is. I had a flirtation with Oriental religion once. I envied the true Buddhists; they were able to reincarnate; not like us – when we're dead, we're dead; this life, that's it – it's the Jewish curse, we don't have heaven or hell and we don't come back – it's now or never. Of course, for me, now is hardly here any more. I'm eighty years old. I find that unforgivable and suddenly it's a millennium

and I stink of the past century, but what can I
do? I'm inching towards dust, and sometimes
I wish it would hurry, preferably in the middle
of a thought, or a sentence, just like that,
although not by a bullet to the forehead. And
then I wonder if anyone will sit shivah for me;
maybe in this bright new twenty-first century
they won't sit shivah any more. Well, the
ultra-Orthodox will, of course, but something
like shivah, in reality, doesn't have much to do
with religion, it's just Jewish. You sit on a
wooden bench for a week, you laugh, cry,
argue as you remember the dead, the
particular dead of this particular shivah, and
you eat a lot, and kvetch a lot, and you get a
sore behind, and it reminds you that you
belong to a people, a race, a culture of sore
behinds and complainers and heated
discussions, of minds in turmoil and minds in
flight and minds exploding like the atom,
which I still don't understand, but it changed
the world, well, it changed the last century, the
world that was, and Albert Einstein came from
the same street in Germany as my second
husband's cousin, what can I tell you? Maybe
this past century will be in fact the next to
last century, and will it all be because a
restless people produce restless minds; when
you don't belong anyplace, your mind doesn't
belong anyplace, you're owned by no one,

except God, and God is only an idea, and so if
you believe in God, you have to believe in
ideas; except now, who believes in God except
the fanatically committed, and if that's true,
who believes in ideas? Now is different,
anyhow; we don't wander any more; we have
a home.

Pause.

I can't catch my breath.

*She tries to control her breath. Her problem is
very quiet, almost unseen, but she can feel it.
She pours a glass of water.*

At my age, breathing is one of the few
pleasures I have left.

She sips the water.

The elderly are supposed to remember the
past with dreadful clarity, but the present –
hardly at all. With me, it's not so true. I have
only vague, wandering images of my

childhood, but yesterday – I remember every
single thing about yesterday. Nothing
happened yesterday. Trust me. But seventy,
seventy-five years ago – Yultishka – a lot
happened, but I'm not so sure what. I see
Yultishka clearly in my dreams; the
subconscious is like an elephant, it never
forgets; but when I'm awake, what do I
remember? Mud roads. Tiny dwellings, I'm
not going to call them houses exactly, but I'm
not going to say huts, so – dwellings. Pink
trees, well, the blossoms were pink. And carts
and wagons. Lots of coming and going;
traffic, I suppose, but no exhaust fumes. We
had an ozone layer then; it's a shame no one
told us, we could have enjoyed it. Yultishka,
just a little pimple on the face of the Ukraine,
you could squeeze it and it would burst. Just
like all the other shtetls, the little Jewish
towns that clung by the side of the larger
Russian communities; well, sometimes
Russian, sometimes Polish; the goyim kept
killing each other and – what do they call it?
– usurping sovereignty.

*Laugh*s.

Sovereignty! The Ukraine! Why would anyone want it? And today? What would it be like today? Yultishka, if it existed still, wouldn't be that far from Chernobyl. But, in 1920, when I was born, it was Russian. There was a civil war going on, as usual, this time just between Russians, Red and White. By the time I was two, there was famine. But there was always a plate on our table. My mother made sure of that. She took in washing, and with the pennies she made from that she bought fruit from a goyisha farmer and sold the fruit from a little stand on the roadside, and with those pennies, she bought us food. I'll tell you the truth, I've never understood why she couldn't buy the food with the money from the washing. How much less was it than the money from the fruit? But that would have been simple and without strain and she wouldn't have been a martyr. My mother was a saint. Everyone in the shtetl said so. Which is very curious, because sainthood is not a Jewish concept. It's not even a Jewish word. She never complained. She never questioned. God had dropped a genuine Christian into the middle of this shtetl and didn't tell anyone. I was born into a contradiction. My mother's milk was never what it seemed. So the saint – Saint Trebele – was the sole support of her family – my older brother, Asher, my little

sister, Rivka, and of course, Rosala, the
middle one, that's me.

Who am I forgetting? Papa. Oh papa! Papa
was tall and actually quite a beauty, especially
his eyes, which were always laughing,
although none of us ever got the joke. Shortly
after Rivka was born, papa announced he was
dying, and took to bed. He was in bed for
years and years. He never stopped dying, but
as far as we could tell, there was nothing
wrong with him. Next to his bed was a large
wardrobe, which was filled with medicine
bottles, most of them empty, and herbal
remedies, most of them used, and none of
them able to cure this mysterious illness,
which was very much like God, there was no
visible sign of it, but some fanatical Jew kept
saying it existed. Doctors used to come from
neighbouring villages – they were always
melancholy – and they brought medicine as
gifts – papa never paid for his hopeless cures
– and people from the surrounding area, not
all of them Jewish, brought him home-made
remedies. He was almost – if you can imagine
this in the Ukraine – a tourist attraction. The
rabbi came and said blessings once a week,
and the effort of listening so exhausted papa
he had to sleep through the next day. And the

village cabbalists came once a week as well
and talked of the devil and mentioned
exorcism, which made papa smile, he had a
soft spot for hocus-pocus. But the saint,
whose religion was more traditional, threw
them out – once a week. Mama truly believed
in goodness; more than that – if you were
Jewish, you had a responsibility to be good;
you were, in fact, put on earth to perpetuate a
moral force. There was only black and white
with her, which, ironically, just made her seem
more Christian.

By the time I was ten I was selling fruit on
the road. Asher taught me to read Russian as
well as Yiddish; I had an ear for languages.
Every day I made new signs describing the
fruit, which did not need description; you
could see them easily enough; melon and
berries were luscious then; I can only imagine
what they're like today in what was once
Yultishka, mutating from fallout. Asher went
to the Yeshiva; it was honourable if a boy
studied. This annoyed me as I had an
overwhelming appetite for knowledge – well,
for most things other than science. I read
everything I could lay my hands on. I fell in
love with words. I memorized large Russian
words and invented new Yiddish ones. I

became pretentious in several languages at once. Asher came home and discussed the Talmud with me; we had discussions and arguments long into the night, the kind girls were not supposed to have, and I learned then that Judaism's greatest contribution to mankind was asking questions that can't be answered, and that the glory of our race has less to do with giving the world Moses and Marx and Jesus, but everything to do with the invention of the phrase 'on the other hand'. The saint was not impressed by our nocturnal discussions, but then nothing seemed to move her, at least not to appreciation. She never kissed us or touched us or teased us; she never said we were good-looking or sweet-natured; she had no pride in us whatsoever; all of her energy was spent in keeping us alive. She hated answering questions; she had to, of course, when I had my first period; she said it was God's curse, in which she was supported by the Bible. Asher, however, said, on the other hand, it might be God's gift, although he never quite explained why, and I said if that were true I'd rather God had just given me a calendar. So I learned an important lesson that night – God's curses are bad enough, but boy, watch out for His gifts. Shortly after that, the Cossacks came. I suppose if you have your first period and your first pogrom within the

same month, you can safely assume childhood
is over.

Years later, a history professor told me they
couldn't have been Cossacks; Stalin has
pacified the Cossacks, he said. Well, there
were a few left over. They had big horses and
big hats and big whips – everything was big –
and beautiful faces; at least that's my memory,
but I'm not sure if my memory is of the actual
event or a scene from the movie *Fiddler on
the Roof* ; in my mind, it's exactly like the
movie, or maybe the movie was exactly like
the event. I close my eyes and I see chorus
boys on horses, there's nothing I can do about
it, but it's hard to reach my age and to have
lived through some of the most tumultuous
events of this century and to make clear
distinctions between reality and the depictions
of reality that constantly surround us.
Actually, they were nicer in life than in the
movie, because they didn't seem to want to
kill anyone, they just wanted to frighten us. It
was a bit like the Ku Klux Klan riding into a
small southern town wearing sheets, except, of
course, I only know that from the movies as
well. And so they rode through the villages
and broke windows and set fire to stores.
They came into our house and we cowered

behind a stove, and they didn't try to harm us, they just smashed everything up and rode away. Asher was shouting, Rivka was crying, I was doing a little of both as befits the middle child. Mama, of course, said nothing. She found a broom. She started cleaning up. It was then that Asher and Rivka and I had the same thought – for in the fuss, there was something we had all forgotten. Papa! We shouted his name. Mama sighed and walked into the bedroom. When she came out she picked up the broom and continued sweeping. Papa's dead, she said. Asher, Rivka and I ran into the bedroom, and we saw that the wardrobe had collapsed on to the bed. Papa's hand was sticking out from under the wardrobe holding an enema bag. We could make out a leg as well, covered with ointments made of rosemary and honey. He had been crushed to death by medicine. Years later, when I became an agnostic, that memory would, just for a second, make me believe in God again.

She sips some water.

Papa's was my first shivah. So many people came we ran out of wooden benches. I think

they needed proof that papa had finally died.
Mama was in her element, totally impassive.
It was God's will.

A few weeks later, on a hot afternoon, I sold
the last grapefruit and went for a walk in the
woods. I came upon a field covered with lilac
trees. I heard a voice. Someone was singing,
singing in an unknown tongue – a gypsy
melody; no, it was Muslim; no, totally
Hebraic; no, wait, I think Spanish, or maybe
African – I couldn't tell – or perhaps it was
from the moon. It summoned lovers and
demons. I crept toward the field. I had to see
who was making this delirious sound. Finally,
I spotted a fragile figure holding on to a tree;
holding, holding and swaying at the same
time. I hid behind a bush and listened to the
melody and suddenly the figure turned, and I
saw its face, covered with sweat and dirt and
desire and longing . . . It was mama. I ran. I
ran into the woods. I ran away from her song.
I ran back to the shtetl. When mama returned
home, she was scrubbed and cool, and she
wore her saintly face. She started to cook.

Pause.

I never thought of her as Christian again. I
had to escape Yultishka. But Asher beat me to
it. He married. From the next village, her
name was Chaya, she was a catch, her family
were merchants, she had even studied at a
school. Her parents gave them money and
with it they moved to Warsaw. Asher left me
with the fruitstand and the sister and the
mother who was really a pagan . . . and each
day I grew a little and each day I died a little,
both at the same time. I did not belong.

I wrote to Asher. I wrote every week. I begged
him to send for me. I begged him to rescue
me. I did not belong. I had fevers, I had a
cold. My ear hurt. I had spots. My nose ran. I
dreamed. I sat in a corner. I watched mama.
Mama ignored me.

Asher wrote and said come. Come, if you can.
He had a child now. Chaya could use help
around the house. Come if you can. He wrote
to mama. Send Rosala to Warsaw. She can
take a train from Kiev. Send her to Warsaw.
Mama looked at me. A dry, cold look. The
same look. Always that look. I was desolate. I
knew there was no money for a train. Mama
went into the bedroom and returned with a

scarf. Orange and blue. Like the scarf of a
magician; wave it and a rabbit appears. There
wasn't a rabbit. There were kopeks instead,
hidden inside. I saved, mama said, for when
it's life or death. But going to Warsaw, Mama,
it's not really life or death. She looked at me.
The same look. Always that look. Yes it is, she
said.

She holds her chest.

Maybe it's in my mind. Maybe there's nothing
wrong with my breathing. Maybe I just panic.
Maybe I should drink some water.

*She pours another glass of water, and begins
to sip it.*

The first time I couldn't catch my breath?
1937. Summer. The café on Krochmalna
Street. Chaos. Prostitutes and artists and
pickpockets and those strange little men who
sold lottery tickets – you could, if you were
lucky, win an American eagle made of
chocolate or three coloured pencils – and
waiters shouting abuse and talk and noise and
the possibility, always, of some kind of

seduction; and though everyone spoke Polish,
and I wasn't yet as fluent as I wanted to be, I
felt almost – not quite – comfortable. Asher
and his friends from the magazine they
worked for were drunk and laughing; Chaya
was in a good mood for once; and the room
seemed to go around and around, as if we
were all in spin-dry. I suppose it was the
wine; we were celebrating my first year in
Warsaw. And then the spin cycle abruptly
stopped and a large man with long red hair
was standing at our table. He looked like a
gypsy, he had a huge earring in his ear, and
his shirt was open, and there was no hair on
his chest – no hair! – every man in Warsaw
was hairy – and he had one perfect blue eye
and one eye of glass, one dead little island in
the middle of such life, and Asher was
introducing him to me, and I knew, without a
doubt, that there would never be anyone else.

We made love that night, surrounded by
canvas; paintings, Yussel's paintings, paintings
of shtetls, of tiny villages with mud roads and
lilac trees; imitation Yultishkas surrounded me
in that garret in Warsaw where I was finally
free and finally a woman. Once when I was a
child I heard the bedsprings in the bedroom
rocking and thumping but there was no other

sound, no human voice; it must have been the
night Rivka was conceived, and I lay in the
front room terrified, terrified by that silence.
But with Yussel and me there was such noise
– moaning and screaming and laughing and
gasping – oh no – no . . .

She waves her hand away.

I don't want to remember.

Pause.

And we lived happily ever after.

She takes a long drink of water.

Yussel wasn't a bad artist. He wasn't exactly a
Chagall, but then, who is? Jews aren't visual –
look at what they wear. I suppose it's because
we were never allowed to reproduce an image
of God, unlike the goyim, who love the naked
bodies of men caught in some kind of sado-
masochistic ecstasy, strung up on a piece of
wood or with an arrow piercing a nipple. But

sex and God are very confused for goyim; for
Jews they're separate. We can't see our God,
so we can't desire Him. And when He
abandons us, as He always does, we feel
betrayed by a parent, not by a lover. Or
maybe, like a parent. One day He just dies.
So, believe me, when I was in bed with
Yussel, there was no religious dimension.
Actually, he was insatiable. He had to have
everything today, as if tomorrow didn't even
exist as a concept. Maybe he knew.

When we weren't making love, we were at the
movies, especially if they showed a western.
We loved cowboys and injuns and canyons
and the Rio Grande and stagecoaches riding
round the bend and tumbleweed rolling into
an empty town – could that have been real?
We liked musicals too, particularly the silly
Yiddish ones, with Molly Picon dancing
around a shtetl, singing –

*Sing*s.

'Yiddle mit a fiddle . . .
Yiddle, Yiddle, Yiddle . . .'

We walked the streets of Warsaw with our
friends, arguing and dreaming and laughing
and the goyim passing by would look at us
with discomfort and even resentment, and one
night, walking across the Kravidjin Bridge, I
heard about Palestine for the first time, the
land of our ancestors, the land that God
promised us, and I giggled, because, even
then, I knew about God's promises. Yussel
would lean over and gently bite my ear and
then nothing else mattered.

Sometimes Yussel would sell a painting, but
he didn't make much of a living; the last thing
he needed was a wife, but now, suddenly, he
had a wife, and a year later, a child. I named
her Esther, she had red hair like her father,
and *two* blue eyes.

I don't know how Yussel lost his eye, he
refused to tell me, but occasionally, in the
middle of the night, he would start to scream
and I would hold him and stroke his brow, and
then Esther would start to cry and I'd have to
go to her, and in the morning he'd accuse me
of deserting him and of not caring about his
pain, and I would say but I don't know what
your pain is, and he would say I was blind,

and I would bite my tongue and not say well, actually, in reality, you're blind, half-blind, and I don't know why. When we made love he would plunge into me, but I could never enter him, not really; emotionally, I was allowed foreplay, nothing else, and I felt, here, in the closest relationship I would ever have, still outside, like that tumbleweed rolling through an empty town, and suddenly I would miss Yultishka and worry about mama and Rivka and then lie awake at night listening to the soldiers marching outside.

When the Nazis first entered Warsaw it didn't mean anything to me. It was someone else's war. I liked Warsaw, but I had no affection for Poland. How much worse could the Germans be? Well, I can't help it, I really did think that, what did I know?

I don't remember the ghetto.

Pause.

Well – OK – packed together. They took us from our homes. They relocated us into one small area and built a wall around us. There

were twelve Jews to a room. Twelve – twelve
– to a room. But I don't remember it. Maybe
it wasn't twelve. I don't know. I'll tell you
what hell is – it's twelve people snoring at the
same time. Maybe I'm imagining it. Yussel
had his bad dreams all the time now. I didn't
have bad dreams. You have to sleep to have
dreams. I was afraid to sleep. I was afraid
something would happen to Esther if I slept.
How had this happened? We had only
yesterday been walking across the Kravidjin
Bridge. We had been in a café just a month
ago eating chocolate cake. Cake. Now there
was a half chicken for the entire room. Twelve
people. Maybe it wasn't twelve. What was
going on? Who was this man with red hair
and an earring? What was I doing with him? I
should have been selling grapefruit on a road.
And then there wasn't a half chicken any
more. We were starving.

I searched for my brother. I found him at the
other end of the ghetto. Asher and Chaya were
living with nine other people. Their child had
died. The cholera. Chaya was screaming when
I entered the room. Asher told me to ignore
her but I couldn't. I tried to comfort her. She
called me a bitch. She pulled my hair. I
slapped her. Soon I was screaming. I don't

know why. They had no food. Asher said he
had contacts who could find me a job in a
factory outside the ghetto. The owner was
friendly to Jews and took in more than she
needed, but only women. Chaya started to beat
her breasts. Asher grabbed a rope and tied her
hands. I saw how thin he was. Why were we
in Warsaw? Chaya started to vomit. The other
people in the room cursed her. I ran out into
the night air. There was no air. Back in my
room, Yussel stared at the ceiling. Esther was
telling herself a story. She was three. We had
a few bread crusts for all of us, for twelve
people. Maybe it wasn't twelve. I took
Yussel's hand. Where were you, why did you
desert me, he said.

I started work at the factory. They let you out
of the ghetto in the morning and escorted you
back at night. Yussel didn't want me to leave,
but we needed the food. It was possible for
women to smuggle scraps of food back into
the ghetto; the young soldiers at the gate were
strangely shy about body searches. One
afternoon, in the factory, we heard noise
coming from the ghetto. We ran to the
window. We could see the ghetto wall. Smoke
was rising behind the wall. We heard
screaming in the distance. Screaming. No, we

didn't. I don't remember what we heard. Some of the factory women fainted. My body lost control. I shat myself. Esther and Yussel were in the ghetto. I ran to the bathroom. Cold water didn't help. I wanted to go to sleep. The screaming grew louder. No, it didn't. I don't remember. We had to go back to our machines.

That night we returned to the ghetto. The streets were filled with bodies. Buildings were burning. SS men were walking with dogs. I found my room; everything in it had been smashed to pieces. It was empty. Where were Esther and Yussel? I walked the streets calling Esther's name, passing other mothers calling the names of their children; a giant chorale of names filled the ghetto under the red sky. Years later someone offered me LSD; I said I didn't have to take it, I knew what it was like, hallucinating; a minute stretched out into an hour, strange visions soaring through your mind and then disappearing, the feeling you will never come back down to reality. I knew what it was like. I found a space where Asher's room had been. It was gone. Asher was gone. Chaya was gone. A hand pulled me off of the sidewalk. It was Simka, a man from our room. He had hidden in a cellar in another part of the ghetto. When the raid began, he was in our room. Yussel had handed Esther to him and said take her to the cellar. But Yussel had stayed behind. How could he slip through the streets unnoticed with his red hair and his earring?

Why did he wear an earring? Did he think he was a gypsy? I wanted to tear it from his ear until the ear bled. He said to Simka, tell her, tell my wife, my Rosala, to protect our daughter. That was it. Thank you very much, Yussel, love of my life. Later someone told me they saw him marching in the left line of prisoners, the line of useless people, the line for one-eyed men, the line that led to the clearing in the wood, where the machine-guns were. Fertilizer. They turned the bodies into fertilizer. What did they do with the earring? I don't remember any of this.

Simka and Esther started running through the streets. Simka did not look at me when he talked. He closed his eyes. He said they passed a soup kitchen. The Jewish Committee were handing out soup. Esther broke away from Simka. Simka covered his face when he talked. Esther ran toward the soup. They had

never distributed soup before. A Ukranian
soldier was passing by. A young blond
Ukranian. Maybe he was a neighbour from
Yultishka. Stalin and Hitler were friends now,
for a minute; the Ukraines helped the
Germans guard the ghetto. But why soup
today? The soldier had a small gun. Simka
said it again and again, a small gun, as if the
size was important. Esther ran for the soup.
The soldier aimed his gun, the small gun.
Esther reached the soup. The soldier pulled
the trigger. I suppose the trigger was small
too. The bullet hit her forehead. He might
have been from Yultishka. He was just passing
by. Simka started to cry. Esther lay dead in
front of the soup. Mostly water, it wasn't
really soup. I kicked Simka in the stomach. I
was supposed to protect her. Thank you very
much, Yussel. Simka fell to the ground. I ran
back into the street. I don't know what
happened next.

Pause.

If I were Buddhist this would give me points.
On account for the next life.

Pause.

It's almost time for my pill. For the breathing.

Pause.

I sat shivah in the sewers. There were no
wooden benches, but God makes allowances.
Except I stopped believing in God. God died
in the ghetto; when I kicked Simka; just about
then. On the other hand, I still needed ritual.
So I sat a kind of mental shivah. For Esther.
For Yussel. For Asher. For mama. For Rivka. I
knew in my heart that mama and Rivka were
gone as well. Later I met someone from a
village near Yultishka who described the end
of our shtetl. The Nazis marched all the Jews
into the schoolhouse, locked the doors, and
burnt it down. Easy. Screams behind the
walls. Again. I sat that kind of shivah for two
years. I don't really know how I got to the
sewers, that's a blank. But once there, oh, I
remember everything. There were about thirty
of us. I was numb. Novocaine. Two years. You
do things to stay alive . . . I remember . . .
everything . . .

*She takes the glass of water and drinks it very
slowly.*

She does not speak.

A long pause.

This I will say. We talked of Jerusalem. We
were by the waters of Babylon, beneath
Warsaw, and we remembered Zion. The
promised land. Promised. Our own. No one
elses. No Cossacks. No Nazis. Just us. Safe.

Well, then. The war was over. One day Nazis
were marching into Warsaw. Another day,
Russians. One day Stalin and Hitler were
buddies. Another day, enemies. It had nothing
to do with us. My mind couldn't absorb facts.
Facts no longer made sense. My head was
filled with images, with jump-cuts. Nothing
was linear. I tried not to have memories. I was
still numb, but my feet worked. I got out of
there. Away from the Russians. I had to go
someplace safe. Where was safe? Oh yes.
Germany was safe. Long lines of refugees,
passing through Poland, rushing toward the
country that destroyed them. That was now
itself destroyed. We passed through Dresden.
A child with no arms crawled through the
streets. The streets were rubble. The goodies
had conquered the baddies, and had saved

what remained of our lives, but the child had
no arms. I found the Americans. They
welcomed us. They gave us cigarettes. I had
never smoked before. I smoked for the next
fifty years. Now I can't catch my breath. They
gave us soup. They put us in a camp. They
called it a centre but, believe me, it was a
camp. A nice camp, not a bad camp, but still,
a camp. Barbed wire and bunk beds. The war
was over. What was I doing in a camp? In
Germany, where it's safe? I was officially
called a displaced person. I could have told
them that a long time before.

The camps were overcrowded. No one knew
what to do with us. We had no homes to
return to. But I had a place to go. I had
Palestine. I was adopted by the Zionists in the
camp. I was a heroine. Hadn't I fought back
in the ghetto? Actually, no. I hadn't; when the
ghetto rose up in its last gasp of fury, I was
already in the sewers. But I let them believe
what they wanted to believe. They were my
ticket out.

One day the smugglers arrived. High-priced
criminals, paid for by the Haganah. They
bribed the soldiers. Two hundred people were

selected from our camp. Some wore three
pairs of clothing on top of one another and
carried a knapsack. I travelled light. I had
nothing. Soap and a towel. We climbed
through a hole in the fence. The soldiers
closed their eyes. The smugglers never smiled.
We climbed into trucks. The trucks sped into
the night. Some people screamed. They
remembered the Nazi trucks. They thought it
was a trick. But the next night we were in
France. In Sete, by the sea. I had never seen
the sea. It was just another image, another
hallucination. A boat was in harbour. It was
falling apart. We were marched aboard, like
cattle, herds of us, mooing and rushing and
falling in the dark. We were being rustled, like
in *Red River* and only caution kept the
smugglers from shouting Yippee-I-O. But
once on board we were no longer cattle. We
were now sardines. If you turned around, your
elbow hit a nose. The boat set sail and secretly
negotiated its way out of the harbour. The
French turned a blind eye. The British were
determined to stop us from going to Palestine.
The British had won Palestine on the
Monopoly board, you see, and they were
trying to hold on both to it and their dignity.
Their foreign minister was named Bevin and
he was the goy from hell. He only allowed
fifteen hundred Jews a month into the Holy

Land; certain basic facts about the war
seemed to have passed him by. The Haganah
were trying to sneak as many Jews as possible
into the country, although sneak is hardly the
word; we were a creaky old boat on the open
seas, difficult to miss, and within a day we
were being tailed by British warships.

The mood on board the boat had changed. We
were allowed on to the open deck and
suddenly there was an accordian and the
sardines were singing and dancing. I heard
melody. The Mediterranean was playful, the
waves hypnotic, and for a moment, the
numbness began to wear away. Then I saw
children throwing a ball, a little girl playing
hide-and-seek, a tiny girl, and I couldn't bear
it. I closed my eyes. I didn't want to
remember. I didn't want the quick sharp
images in my brain and I was angry at Yussel,
at Yussel, for wearing an earring.

I opened my eyes. I saw a man's chest, a
hairless chest. What was the point of opening
my eyes if the images remained? Then I
realized the chest was attached to a sailor who
was smiling at me. Why was he smiling at
me? There was a chill from the sea. He put on

his shirt, but he was clumsy, and he put his
head into the hole for his arm, and he was
stuck. The ship was run by sailors who
couldn't navigate a shirt. Suddenly my body
was seized by convulsions. My spine went
into spasm, my stomach jumped. I felt an
electric current run through my bosom, and I
knew this was it, finally, I was going to die,
and I heard a sound from my throat, a strange,
heaving sound, and then I realized what was
happening. I was laughing. I had forgotten. I
hadn't laughed since the café on Krochmalna
Street. Something Yussel had said. He kissed
my cheek which was wet from tears of
laughter. Had that really happened? And now,
in another life, on the open sea, this silly
sailor with his head in the armhole had made
my body scream ha-ha-ha. Who invented that
sound, those syllables? If ha-ha-ha is a word,
it's the only one that exists in every language.
And then the sailor – he who produced
ha-ha-ha – winked at me and disappeared into
the crowd.

He returned that evening. We were still on the
open deck. He sat beside me, or rather, fell
beside me; he tripped on a rope holding a pail
of water and splashed the water over us. We
were squeezed together, refugees on either

side. He was flirting with me, at least I think
he was; I had no experience of flirting; Yussel
was very direct – that first night at the café he
said I think we should fuck and I blushed but
I thought so too and what was the point of
pretending otherwise? The sailor's name was
Sonny. Sonny Rose. He spoke Yiddish, his
parents were from a village not far from mine,
but he was born in America. Most of the
sailors were American volunteers. None of
them had experience on a boat, but they too
had dreams of Palestine. They didn't have to
be on the ship; we did; and that made me like
him. I asked if he was from the West, with
Indians and tumbleweed, but he said no, New
Jersey. I liked him a little less. When I told
him my name he said oh what a shame, we
can never marry, you would be Rose Rose.
I'm not sure that my face showed it, but in
some way, I think I smiled.

Mr Bevin didn't smile, though. His warships
moved closer. Someone said they were
destroyers. The next morning the sailors hung
a flag across the top of the boat. It had the
Star of David on it. And a sign as well, a sign
that renamed the ship. It said: *Exodus 1947*. I
can see that sign so clearly. But, of course,
how could I then, standing underneath it? Am

I remembering the newsreels or the movie
with Paul Newman? Or did I crank my neck?
How can I tell? Sonny helped put the sign up,
but he lost his footing, and dangled from the
Star of David until his laughing shipmates
helped him down.

We were nearing land, promised land. Only
nearing, we were still in international waters,
which were supposedly safe. That night the
warships moved to our side. They squeezed
us. Then they rammed us. We heard English
voices on megaphones. What were they
saying? Then there was tear gas. British
sailors wearing steel helmets boarded the boat.
They had clubs. We had soda pop. The
Haganah had loaded our hardest food supplies
on deck for us to fight with. Refugees were
hurling cans of kosher corned beef at the steel
helmets. I saw one of the sailors being
clubbed. I saw a boy, only sixteen, his family
wiped out in the camps, shot in the face. He
died with Palestine on his lips. I picked up a
potato. I threw the potato. Suddenly
everything that had happened in the past seven
years released itself through potatoes. I was
no longer numb. I threw potatoes for my child,
I threw potatoes for Yussel, for mama. I was
screaming. I was exhilarated. I was almost

happy. And my aim was good. I was wiping
out Mr Bevin's Boys. I saw someone aim a
gun at me, and then suddenly I was on the
ground. Sonny had thrown me down. A bullet
whizzed above us. Sonny dragged me into a
corner, away from the fighting. He kissed me.
His lips tasted of flesh. Yussel's tasted of
cherry vodka. I've just saved your life, he
said. I looked at him. I hated him for it.

The British had the boat, rather the hulk, the
remains of the boat. The Royal Navy towed us
into the harbour. We were entering Palestine at
last, but we were under arrest. We started to
sing 'Hatikvah'. Listen, 'Hatikvah' is not
exactly the 'Marseillaise'; like most national
anthems it goes on too long and no one knows
the words. So we made up words. Then we
heard the real words coming from the shore.
Jewish settlers were waiting for us on the
dock and they were singing. Our voices
blended together. It was yet another
hallucination, another LSD trip, except this
one had a musical score. Sonny grabbed my
hand. He was crying. All the Americans were
crying. But the refugees didn't cry. We were
too tired. Was it ever going to end?

We landed. The mandate police came on
board and took us off the boat in single lines.
Goodbye, sardines, back to cattle. Palestine
didn't seem like much. It was dirty and hot
and there were insects everywhere and
strange-looking Arabs in robes and headgear
and camels and jeeps and the settlers cheering
us as we marched by and suddenly the woman
in front of me fell to the ground and kissed
the earth and screamed Palestine, and I
thought what a sentimental fool she was, and
then I felt dirt grazing my chin and I realized
I was on the ground too and my lips were
touching the dirt and I thought the earth tasted
of cherry vodka but that was in my mind and
I didn't know why I was on the ground or why
I had started to cry and I felt a policeman pull
me up and march me back into the line.

We were hungry, but they didn't feed us. We
were thirsty, but they didn't offer us water.
Instead they sprayed us for lice. For years
after I thought if the British invite you to their
house they spray you first. And then they
marched us to another ship and we sailed
away from Palestine. It had been a mirage,
five hours in the Promised Land, a stopover
on the cruise ship, a quick package tour to
salvation. Now we were headed for Cyprus,

where they had – guess what? – camps, camps for illegal immigrants. The Americans were on our boat as well and the next morning Sonny, who understood a compass, realized we were not sailing to Cyprus after all. We were on the open seas, heading back to Europe.

Sonny was agitated. *The Exodus* had created a scandal. The entire world was watching us, he said. There were even reporters on board. He didn't stop talking. Why was he talking to me? Why didn't he talk to someone else? He was boring me. I didn't care about a propaganda victory. I just wanted to sleep. In a bed, near mama. I wanted mama. Why didn't he stop talking? He kept taking my hand. I let him. It didn't matter.

We landed in a French port. The French said they would only allow volunteers to disembark. No one volunteered. The Haganah smuggled messages on to the ship saying Do Not Leave. Why would we leave? Where did we have to go? We were taking a stand. I wanted a bed. I didn't care. It was so hot. We were sailing again. We were sardines again. The constant changing from fish to cow and back again had broken my spirit, which had

only half existed anyhow, and then only
because of Palestine. It was so hot. The
reporters filed their dispatches – a homeless
people wander from port to port. Mr Bevin
had a shit fit. He sent our boat back to
Germany. Sonny kept talking. He said the
British had overplayed their hand, they had a
public relations disaster. I looked at him,
stupified; if you have just been through a war
in Europe, not to mention a Holocaust, you
weren't exactly sure what public relations
meant.

We landed again, this time in Hamburg. We
refused to disembark. British soldiers burst on
to the ship and clubbed us; they were getting
quite good at that, and dragged us off of the
boat. They took us to a train. A woman
screamed when she saw the train had barred
windows. I was hustled on to the train. It was
chaos. I didn't see Sonny, but he was
American, so he was free. Suddenly there was
a lot of steam; the train started to move, very
slowly. I saw Sonny on the platform running
alongside the train shouting my name. I went
to the door which was still open. This is
ridiculous, he shouted. Jump off the train.
Jump off and marry me. I'll take you to

America. And then later we can go to
Palestine. Jump. Rose! Jump!

I didn't know what to do. My heart was barely
alive; if my body jumped, it wouldn't bring
love with it. And maybe I still had a husband.
After all, how did I really know that Yussel
was dead? Someone saw him marching to the
machine-guns, sure, but did they see a body?
On the other hand, how could he have
survived? But shouldn't I search for him? Just
in case? In case of what – a miracle?

Jump, he screamed. The train was leaving the
platform. The train to nowhere. At least I
think it was leaving. Or was this too a movie?
How many times had I watched this scene
with the steam and the platform and the lover?
Maybe we were still on the boat. America, he
cried. I leaned out of the train. I couldn't
believe I had a future. America, America! My
mind closed down. I shut my eyes. What did it
matter? I jumped. He caught me and then
dropped me and we rolled over on the
platform and then we were surrounded by
soldiers with guns and they were shouting at
us and I watched the train disappear into the

mist, into Europe, into what years later my
kind would call The Old Country.

*She takes a bag from beneath the wooden
bench. She removes a group of medicine
bottles from the bag, and lays them, one by
one, on the bench.*

Papa would be proud. I take medicine now.
For the breathing. For the cholesterol. For the
kidney. For this and that. I'm doing what papa
dreamed of for so long. I'm dying. Not
specifically, but when you're eighty you are,
in essence, on the way out. Isn't it strange that
I'm still alive? How many times I closed my
eyes and said now, now, take me now, please. I
can't go on. If there is a God, you'll take me
now, and in a moment like that I believed in
Him, and then when I opened my eyes, I
didn't. But God is like a policeman, He's
never there when you want him, and then, of
course, He arrests you when you're innocent.
Why do I spend so much time talking about
something I don't believe in?

The problem is I can't swallow pills. Once I
choked on an aspirin and almost died and
that's not how I want to go, I want to go

quietly in the middle of a sentence. So I've
been frightened of pills ever since. I envy
people who just throw their head back and
drop a whole bunch of capsules down their
throat. And then swallow and smile. Bastards.
So I chew my pills. The problem is they taste
like donkey droppings. So I have to kill the
taste.

*She takes a container of ice cream out of her
portable feezer and puts it on her lap. She
opens it. She chews a pill, and then eats a few
spoonfuls of ice cream, and repeats the
process as she talks, until she has finished her
medicine.*

Peanut butter vanilla. It's a new flavour. I like
to be au courant. I know, I know, I'm eating
ice cream to take a pill for cholesterol. I'll tell
you something – who cares?

The first time I ate ice cream was in Atlantic
City. Ice cream and frozen custard. There was
a frozen-custard stand on the boardwalk, in
front of the burlesque house, near the pier,
across from the beach, where I sold chairs.
Sonny was born and raised in Atlantic City.
I'm sure he told me that on the boat, but I

usually wasn't listening to him, and as a
result, I knew nothing about him. Or maybe
he told me during the endless days when we
argued with the soldiers and the immigration
officials and the bureaucrats; the days of
filling out forms, when all I could think of
was why am I here, shouldn't I have stayed on
the train, who is this man? The Americans
were nice to us, though; Sonny had an uncle
in some bureau and finally I received a paper
that said I existed, and a Jewish chaplain
married us in Berlin, and then I was back on a
boat, with a husband who was seasick all the
time, which he wasn't on *The Exodus*, and I
nursed him and asked myself who – who is
he?

Sonny's parents had a few 'who' questions of
their own. Their boy runs away to be a pirate
and returns with a catatonic shtetl girl, when
what they always wanted was a nice Jewish-
American daughter-in-law named Sheila or
Arlene, who at the very least spoke English,
which is a little weird if you ask me, as they
had never bothered to learn the language
themselves, whereas I became fluent within a
year. But if his parents still spoke Yiddish
they were hardly alone; Atlantic City was
Warsaw-on-the-Sea, which was ironic because

if ever a people were not built for bathing
suits it was ours. The air smelled of aspirin
and chicken fat and suntan oil, but the Jews
who made the city their summer playground
were the fortunate ones; they had had the
good sense to leave Europe when the going
was good. But guilt hung in the sea air as
well, and my presence disturbed them. They
were relieved to discover I did not have a
number on my arm, but they certainly weren't
interested in the images in my brain. They
didn't want to know. Not that I wanted to tell
them. Once I overheard a woman say, These
people go on too much about the past; life
isn't easy for anyone. She was wearing a mink
coat and it was July. She was a guest at one of
the many palaces that pretended they were
hotels, palaces from another age, a jazz age, a
Scott Fitzgerald age, beautiful and hideous at
the same time. The same minked woman was
heard saying, Art deco, art shmeco, the
bathrooms are clean. For one dollar a boy
pushed you on a rolling chair on the
boardwalk – a rolling chair was a chair that
rolled, all the terms in Atlantic City were
literal – and you passed the shmeco palaces
and the dancing waters – coloured water that
sprouted in different formations and thus
danced – and the Steel Pier, which had two
movie theatres, a vaudeville house, a dance

hall and a diving horse, which was, needless
to say, a horse that dived into the ocean. You
passed the Ice Capades, an ice show that spent
each summer in Atlantic City and was thought
exotic because ice-skating was one of those
useless things that only goyim did. You passed
the arcades and the fortune-tellers and the
stores selling salt-water taffy, which ruined
Jewish teeth for the next two generations.
Sonny took me on a rolling chair on my first
night, and halfway down the boardwalk we
passed a store selling nuts and suddenly we
were approached by a six-foot peanut with a
huge peanut head who danced over to our
rolling chair and kissed me on the forehead
and called me little lady and I knew then that
I was foolish to think my hallucinations would
end when I arrived in America and I wondered
if I had survived the sewers of Warsaw so I
could be groped by a giant peanut. Why
hadn't I stayed on the train and returned to a
nice sensible displaced person camp?

Sonny's father owned several beach chair
concessions and he gave one to Sonny as a
start up the ladder – that was an American
expression – although I couldn't imagine what
beach chairs would lead to. We rented our
beach chairs by the hour to the sunburned

crowds; Sonny and I would schlep the chairs
to a designated spot in the blazing heat, which
often meant Sonny tripped over a chair, both
of them flying in several directions at once.
He never wore a shirt on the beach, which
was a saving grace, although his body lacked
Yussel's sharp lines. Yussel's this, Yussel's
that, Yussel's report card had straight As,
whilst Sonny's was barely average. At night
there were attempts at lovemaking although he
was as clumsy in bed as he was on solid
ground, and I tried not to think of Yussel's
penis and I wished the stranger on top of me
wasn't called Sonny because I couldn't even
help him out by faking love-talk when he had
the name of a child. Our lovemaking was
silent, like my parents', and in the morning I
was sullen and distant and cruel. When I
became pregnant, I panicked. How could I
have another child, a child I wouldn't be able
to protect? I thought of throwing myself down
the stairs, but I could never act on my baser
instincts, and so Abner was born. Sonny
wanted me to name him Asher, but how could
I say Asher every day and remember? Abner
was close enough, and it was so American, it
could even be the name of a cowboy.

Sonny and I still dreamed of Palestine, except
it was no longer Palestine, but Israel, a nation
at last, thanks to some degree to *The Exodus*.
The adventures of our pathetic boat had
swung world opinion in favour of creating a
new state. We knew we belonged there, but I
couldn't face another long journey, not just
yet. For once in my life I wanted to stay put,
if only for a few years.

Sometimes we would go out at night. There
was the Harlem Follies at the Jockey Club,
and the burlesque house, which was fun,
mainly because the comedians were Jewish
and told Jewish jokes. But then the comedians
on television were Jewish as well, and Yiddish
words entered the English language, words
like schmuck and schlep and schmatte and
schmooze and chutzpah. We saw Yiddish
magicians at the hotels who pulled little
Jewish rabbits out of their hats and we heard
chazanas, female cantors who sang
melancholy shtetl melodies and I would
remember the lilac tree and finally
understand. Molly Picon came once to
entertain; she was tiny and depressingly
energetic and she sang 'Yiddle mit a Fiddle'
as if she were still simulating shtetl life on a
Warsaw screen.

We went to the Yiddish theatre and saw plays
in which demons and goblins haunted the
shtetls, and I remembered how superstitious
we were in Yultishka, how mama would spit
three times if anyone mentioned the dead and
how Satan was as accepted a presence as God.
One night we saw *The Dybbuk*, a play about a
young girl whose body is possessed by the
soul of her dead lover. I was trembling as the
curtain came down. What's wrong, Sonny
asked. I didn't answer. I couldn't bear to look
at him. I ran out on to the boardwalk and then
on to the beach and stared at the ocean which
was bathed in moonlight. I could run into the
sea and find that spot where the horizon
ended. Sonny rushed to me and took me in his
arms. No, there's another answer, I thought. I
would bring Yussel back to me. I would make
Yussel's spirit possess my body.

If Yussel was really going to possess me, I
needed to give him a push. I decided to dye
my hair red and wear one long gypsy earring
as well as trousers, which was not an accepted
fashion for women in those days. Some kind
of prudence prevented me from gouging out
one eye. I expected Sonny's parents would be
outraged by my new appearance, but instead
they approved. They thought I looked less

Russian, which was a good thing, as, thanks
to Senator McCarthy, Russian was definitely
out of fashion, and my old more severe look
was suspicious. The hysteria over reds under
beds was in high gear and actually communist
was just a code word for Jew. One
congressman even made a speech in the
House Of Representatives claiming that
communists had betrayed and then killed
Jesus, which was, as metaphors go, not too
subtle. As Americans were no longer very
good on horses, they conducted their pogroms
around committee tables and under television
lights. I wasn't too concerned about myself; I
knew that the politicians were mesmerized by
the state department and show business; I
didn't think they were panicked about the
beach chair industry. Still, Sonny's parents
were relieved when I assumed my non-
Russian madwoman look. This annoyed me
because one of the points about possession is
that everyone around you recognizes it.
Yussel's persona within me was still only skin-
deep.

He needed inducement. I found a book about
Cabala and in it the perfect magic spell for
summoning a dead spirit. It involved semen,
which was tricky, but finally one night, as

Sonny fumbled inside of me, I asked him to
pull out and come on my stomach. As soon as
he had finished I jumped out of bed and
scooped up his semen on a piece of
cardboard. I ran to the kitchen where I mixed
the semen with a chopped chicken neck and
olive oil and cloves. Sonny stood in the
doorway, watching. I knew he would never
forgive me. Instead, he smiled in a way I
hadn't seen before. My fascination with his
semen was seemingly a boon to his manhood,
and my dalliance with a magic potion was so
– well – not American, so primitive, so
European, so exotic, and after all, isn't that
why he had married me and not Stephanie
Perlow from Asbury Park? I smeared the
potion on the bedroom door. Sonny then
offered to assist me, little dreaming he was
helping me summon my first husband. But
Yussel was curiously uninterested in Sonny's
semen; I yearned to have him inside my body,
but he just wasn't there yet.

Maybe if I behaved like Yussel it would give
him a push in my direction. I started to
swagger around the house and I took up
painting and once, when Sonny returned from
Abner's room where he had been reading him
a story, I accused him of deserting me.

Sonny's joy was uncontained; he thought I had
missed him. OK, I thought, maybe it would
help if I noticed women. I remembered
walking with Yussel on Grabowska Street
which was near the Muranow Theatre and
always filled with young actresses. Yussel
insisted I walk on his left, so if I looked at
him sideways I would only see his glass eye;
supposedly I would be unaware that his good
eye was checking out every pretty girl that
passed. Yussel was never faithful. I didn't
admit that then, but now that I was almost
him, I knew it was so. Who had he slept with?
Were they friends of mine? If only Yussel
would come into my body and name names,
as if he were in front of Senator McCarthy.
One night I placed my hand on Sonny's sister-
in-law's right breast. I knew at that moment I
had gone too far and the entire family would
know that Yussel was trying to return. But his
sister-in-law was thrilled; she asked me to
meet her the next day on the boardwalk by the
cotton-candy stand. The more I became like
Yussel, the more everybody liked me. Yussel
had become the most popular woman in
Atlantic City. But still he eluded me. He
wasn't inside.

So then Miss America arrived. The Miss
America Pageant officially ended the summer
season in Atlantic City and it was a big deal
for the beach chair trade since the pageant
began with a parade. The beauty queen of
every state rolled down the boardwalk on an
individual float and, thank God, onlookers had
to sit on something. You booked one of our
chairs a month in advance, it was that popular.
All the ladies from the hotels put on their best
summer dresses and oohed and ahhed over the
pretty shiksas. The parade began with a little
band and then the first girl, Miss Alabama; it
was alphabetical. People cheered and whistled
and were especially excited if the girl was
from their home state; and the perky little
Protestant faces glided slowly by.

Abner was playing in and around the chairs;
he was three, the dangerous age, the age of
Esther, but I felt he was safe as both Yussel
and I were looking after him. Yussel wasn't
inside of me yet, but he was close. I was
convinced he was somewhere in the vicinity. It
was a blazing hot day. Sonny decided to buy
us cream sodas. He crossed over the
boardwalk, in front of Miss Colorado, and
disappeared into the crowd. I lay back and
closed my eyes. I opened them, saw Miss

Delaware, closed them again. Yussel was so
close. I knew it. I'm sure he was enjoying the
parade. So many pretty girls. Bastard. I began
to drift. I awoke to hear Abner screaming
daddy, daddy. I looked across the boardwalk,
as Miss Iowa waved to me. Sonny was
lurching through the crowd on the other side.
He was holding three cans of cream soda. He
dropped one can. He picked it up. He dropped
another. He lost his balance. He stepped on a
woman's foot. She screamed. He dropped the
third can. People were laughing at him. He
started to cross to us, but he lurched again
and collided with Miss Massachusetts, or
rather, the bottom of her float. He was down
for the count. Miss Massachusetts didn't miss
a beat, she just kept waving and smiling and
ignoring the funny man sprawled on the
ground. Someone in the crowd shouted the
guy's drunk. But I knew that wasn't true;
Sonny never touched alcohol. And, then, in a
flash, it happened. What I had been waiting
for. The Miracle. I felt a shudder near my
heart. Someone was pushing his way into my
body. It was Yussel. Yussel had come at last.
Yussel had taken possession. Miss New
Hampshire looked at me as she went past; had
she seen Yussel dive inside of me? In the
distance I saw Miss New York and I wondered
if she would shout dybbuk, dybbuk. The

crowd applauded. But it wasn't as I imagined.
I thought I would hear Yussel's voice, perhaps
even speak with his voice, and certainly, I
would think his thoughts. But no, he took
possession with his eye. He entered my own
eyes and they saw through his one good one.
My eyes – Yussel's eye – brought Sonny into
sharp focus and saw that Sonny wasn't
clumsy, after all, and Sonny certainly wasn't
drunk. Yussel's eye saw that Sonny was ill,
that Sonny had some kind of disease, that
Sonny was now maybe dying. I took a deep
breath. I ran to Sonny and helped him up.
Don't know what's wrong, sweetheart, he said.
It's nothing, it's just the sun, I said, but inside
of me, inside, I said Yussel – goodbye,
because I knew that now he had to leave and
leave for ever, and I felt his good eye release
its hold on my brain and I felt his spirit lift up
through my body and out of my body and fly
over Miss Oregon and Miss Pennsylvania and
fly further still until it was over the Steel Pier
and its diving horse and fly even further until
it had disappeared into the humid New Jersey
air.

Pours another glass of water.

What's the point of taking a pill if it doesn't
help? I think my pills are made of sugar. My
doctor says there's no problem with my
breathing. If there was, he says, I wouldn't
talk so much. You'll drop dead talking, he
says. He's trying to frighten me. Believe me,
it's an inducement.

Sips the water.

OK. So. Eight years later I owned a hotel in
Miami Beach. Well, that's America, isn't it?
Go figure. What could I do? I had a husband
who required a lot of medical care. Americans
tend to think of illness as unhealthy. It costs.
So I had to go out and hustle. I took a job
ordering food for the Majestic Hotel. Soon I
was running the kitchen. Soon I was
managing the place. The guests loved me. I
understood them and their complaints and I
was pleasant when I had to be and cruel when
it was necessary and it was easy because it
allowed me to protect Sonny, and Abner as
well, and I could do for them what I failed to
do for Esther. Maybe that's why Yussel's eye
had showed me the truth. Maybe. Who knows.
Sonny's was a rare neurological disorder; it
had been building slowly through the years –

when he fell at my feet on the ship he was not
only manifesting love – and now it would
accelerate. Motion, speech and thought would
slowly disintegrate. The doctors could do
nothing. Sonny was as devastated by the
knowledge of the disease as the disease itself.
Cigarettes became his passion, his profession,
his art form. He sat at the kitchen table. He
would drop a cigarette on the table, pick it up,
drop it again, pick it up – the table became a
mosaic of burns and the burns represented
some kind of pleasure. Sometimes I gave him
sexual relief. I wanted to surround him with
an illusion of love.

Our dreams, our fantasies, about Israel had
started to grow again before my obsession
with the dybbuk, but now they had to be
tucked away, like Sonny's personality, into a
distant closet. Abner grew; we called him
Abbie now; and by the time he was seven his
thin little voice would make the evening
announcement over the Majestic loudspeaker
– The dining room is now open for dinner –
as the dining-room doors flung open to a
stampede; it was every man for himself as the
hotel guests desperately rushed toward that
evening's special brisket or smoked whatever.

The guests were intrigued by me because of
The Exodus. That gave me cachet; it spelled
adventure, unlike the death camps, which were
still too dark and threatening to be thought
about. A boat they could deal with. I didn't
tell them about anything else. Nor did I tell
Abbie about the ghetto, or even Yultishka. I
made sure that the guests never spoke directly
to him in Yiddish. I wanted Abbie to be an
all-American boy. I obsessively devoured
books during the night, but kept that a secret
vice. I no longer dressed like a demented
gypsy. My suddenly tasteful wardrobe stood
out from the clashing colours favoured by the
Majestic clientele. They knew I didn't quite
belong. But what finally cemented my
popularity was the one true gift that Sonny
had given me, if you don't count my life, and
that was my name. Who could forget Rose
Rose?

What people did forget was Majestic. Soon
they were saying we're going to Rose Rose's
for the summer. That is, those who still came
to Atlantic City. There were now black ghettos
surrounding the hotel strip, and since victims
of prejudice seem susceptible to the disease
themselves, Atlantic City just packed up and
moved to Florida. The Jersey shore was

desolate; Mr Peanut stopped dancing, as did
the coloured waters; the burlesque house
closed, and salt-water taffy became extinct.

The owner of the Majestic, Mr Feldstein,
asked me to become his partner in a new hotel
in the booming Sunshine State. He couldn't
afford to lose Rose Rose. So the Double Rose
Hotel opened on Collins Avenue. We promised
double the comfort, double the sea air, and
our old Majestic customers came flocking.
The dining room was once again open for
dinner, only further south. And every so often,
Abbie and I would turn on the television on
our tropical veranda in Miami Beach and
watch, on the news, an abandoned palace-
hotel in Atlantic City being demolished. The
boardwalk was littered with rubble, like the
streets of Dresden, where I once saw a child
with no arms.

*Takes a long drink of water and then puts it
down, refreshed.*

Each summer a group of young Israelis came
to our hotel and gave us a presentation. It's
unfair to say that they were aglow with youth,
because it was so much more than that; there

was a passion and belief in the future that I
had not encountered before. Future wasn't
even a concept in Yultishka or Warsaw or even
in Atlantic City or Miami; on some
subconscious level we knew we were skipping
over quicksand. But the Israelis seemed to
lack subconscious; they were entirely up front
and present with no dark or hidden corners.
They showed us slides of their kibbutz, they
sang and danced the hora and collected money
from our guests and each time they urged us
to follow them back to join them in their great
adventure and each time I wanted to, I wanted
to be on the edge again, I wanted to dangle
over a crevice with a very slender rope, but
now I was a Rose Rose with responsibilities,
so instead I gave money to plant trees in the
names of my family. It seemed fitting to make
mama into a tree, although they couldn't
promise me lilac. Abbie made friends with the
Israelis, especially a young couple named
Noam and Rutie, and when he was sixteen I
let him spend the summer on their kibbutz. He
left with acne and returned with a clear
complexion and I knew he had discovered not
only olive groves and irrigation ditches but
sex as well.

Two summers later Egypt invaded Israel.
Abbie begged me to give him the air fare to
Tel Aviv. How could I refuse? His father was
only a few years older when he ran off to *The
Exodus*. Abbie went to Noam's kibbutz and
worked in the fields while the men were away.
It famously took Israel six days to win the
war. It was unreal. Miami Beach was jubilant.
We had an all-night party at the Double Rose.
We were all warriors. There would be no
screams behind a wall again. *The Exodus*
would not be towed away again. I cried that
night as I hadn't in years, but I wasn't sure
why. Abbie phoned me. He wanted to stay. I
wasn't surprised.

I told Sonny our child was living on a
kibbutz; that he had, in essence, achieved our
dream for us. Sonny's hands shook, his eyes
were vacant, the nurse fussed. Did he
understand how the world had changed? A
few months later his heart gave up. I sat
shivah and mourned not his death but his life.

Abbie returned for the funeral and promptly
fell in love with a young nurse from Sonny's
hospital. She was blonde and sweet and, as her
name was Kim, definitely not Jewish. One of

Christianity's more interesting contributions to twentieth-century culture was names like Kim. Abbie stayed on to court her, and soon Kim was as much in love with Abbie's dream as Abbie himself. She took instruction and converted to Judaism and changed her name to Chava and they were married under a chuppah at the Double Rose and soon, as if it hadn't happened at all, they were gone.

I was alone. My husband was dead, my son was gone. Sonny had been a vegetable for years, but at least he was my vegetable. Abbie stopped listening to me some time ago, but it was my voice he was ignoring. Now there was silence. Not even the sewers were silent – rats make noise. People talked all the time in the hotel, but their sounds blended and I heard nothing.

Except for Bessie Goodman. I heard Bessie Goodman because she never spoke. She drove the staff crazy. It was the styrofoam boxes, I imagine. Bessie placed her meals – three meals a day – into styrofoam boxes. Well, most of her meals. She did nibble a little in the dining room, but only a little, and then – woosh – food into box. Coffee as well; liquid didn't faze her. She kept the boxes in a small freezer in her room. Soon there were too many boxes for the freezer. Her room became a shrine to decaying chopped liver and gefilte fish. I didn't have to ask why; I saw The Old Country stamped on her brow. She was storing supplies. I sat with her in her room, in absolute silence. We both knew. But Mr Feldstein anticipated a health crisis and he sent for her son.

Morton Goodman arrived at the hotel with a group of friends. They wore outrageous colours and beads and they all had musical instruments. They were, in fact, a band. The name of the band was MORT and they sang about death, a subject they knew nothing about. To them, death was what you did after life. MORT went to Bessie's room and played for her. They sang their entire repertoire. Finally she couldn't take it any longer. She threw out the styrofoam boxes. MORT emerged victorious.

Morton thanked me for being kind to his mother. He took my hand. His shirt was open and I noticed his chest was smooth. Uh-oh.

He was twenty-eight. I was forty-eight, big
deal, barely old enough to be his mother . . .

Laughs.

Oh well. We became lovers. I started wearing
beads. I bought a guitar. The hotel guests
became restive. Bessie Goodman started
losing weight. I threw away my bra. Mr
Feldstein suggested I took a few months'
leave. It would be good for my head. What a
hip phrase, I thought.

I went to Connecticut and moved into a
commune with Morton and his friends. There
were twelve of us in an empty loft. We
smoked a lot of dope and talked about peace
and love and noble things and I did not
mention the last time I lived twelve to a room
lest I blacken their innocence. They called me
Cool Mama and Morton wrote a song for me.
'Rose Is A Rose'. He claimed not to have
heard of Gertrude Stein. There were long
conversations into the night, intense and
blurry; as if Asher and his fellow Yeshiva
students were high on marijuana. I didn't have
to hide my obsessive reading habits from
them, as I did at the hotel. I felt free to enjoy

language within a new culture that was, in its
own way, destroying it.

Almost everyone in the commune was Jewish
but that seemed to play no part in their
identity. We discussed Buddha and karma
instead of Rabbi Emanuel of Minsk, we went
to ashrams instead of shul, and recited
mantras instead of kaddish. Morton and I went
away to meditate, to an ashram run by Ran To
Poy, the former Seymour Goldstein. I tried to
empty my mind. I couldn't. Nothing in my
background prepared me not to think, not to
question, not to somehow confuse the issue.
My past kept floating through my head. I
didn't welcome the memories but I couldn't
pretend they didn't exist and I couldn't
pretend I wasn't Jewish. It was just some kind
of DNA in my bones. I left Ram To Poy and I
left Morton. I told him I was too old. He
thought I meant age. I couldn't explain. Mr
Feldstein welcomed me back with a relieved
grin. He was a kind man. Two years later, I
married him.

Abbie and Chava had a family. Rafi first, then
Irit, then Doron, beautiful children, born with
the olive features of their land, as if the earth

itself had conceived them. I went to visit. My
first time since I kissed the ground. It wasn't
like my memory. I fell in love with the land,
with the desert and the hills and the amazing
sense of green, green planted by pioneers,
green transforming an arid earth. I loved too
the feeling that everyone, absolutely everyone,
in the country looked like my relative; even,
in some odd way, the unamused faces in the
small Arab villages we drove hurriedly
through; there was something in their eyes
that I recognized, a look I remembered from
the sardines on *The Exodus*. When I arrived at
the airport, Abbie said Welcome home, Mama,
and of course he was right. It was home, and I
cried when he said it, and I cried when I left,
two weeks later, for Miami Beach and my
husband and my hotel.

Actually, the hotel wasn't doing so well. Many
of our customers had died; others were now
too old to have anything to take a vacation
from. The neighbourhood had changed as
well; it had suddenly become Cuban, with
loud salsa music, which was nice, and cocaine
dealers, which wasn't. I suggested we convert
the hotel into a retirement home; our guests
could just stay on for ever, and end their days
quietly by the sea, albeit to a Latin beat, with

the occasional sound of bullets to spice up the
night air. We redecorated and hired nurses and
Double Rose was in business again. Mr
Feldstein and I had our own apartment nearby;
he was an amiable companion, and he knew to
leave me alone when I had my moods, when,
once or twice a year, I would retreat into my
room and wonder why I went to the factory
that day so long ago. But eventually, I would
play 'Rose Is A Rose' on my Walkman –
MORT had become successful and the song a
hit – and I would think how strange it all was
and then open my door and return to a
semblance of life.

Every summer I returned to Israel. It was
changing. The milk was slightly sour, the
honey a bit tart. There was a war on, a few
miles away, in Lebanon, and Jews were being
killed again, but this time Jews were killing as
well, and we weren't really sure if it was in
self-defence, and we saw photographs of
women and children picking their way through
the rubble and the rubble wasn't ours, it was
next door, and we were confused, and our
little boys had grown and started a beard and
had wet dreams and carried a gun and
marched down the road into another land.
Abbie and his friends on the kibbutz hated it.

Noam and Rutie were in despair; they were
sabras, after all, they had virtually created this
land, but not for this, they said, not for this.
Chava, however, was fervently in favour of the
war. Chava/Kim had the passion of the
converted. She knew what the Bible said
about enemies. She became increasingly
religious. She began to keep a kosher house.
She cut off her hair and wore a wig. Abbie
was appalled then confused then hostile. The
kibbutzniks and the religious despised each
other. I did not really understand. Abbie and
Chava did not look for common ground; they
pushed each other away. Their house was
choking with tension.

One day a theatre in Haifa brought a play to
the kibbutz. It was a play designed for a
young audience and indeed it was about
teenagers in the Warsaw ghetto. Rafi, Irit and
Doron wanted me to go with them. I had no
desire to revisit the ghetto, even in make-
believe. Enough already. But I did want my
grandchildren to understand our past. OK, I
thought, knowledge is more important than
pain, so I went.

The auditorium was filled with eager young
faces. Onstage was an imitation ghetto, a little
too pretty, a little too tidy. There was no
stench. It was utterly foreign to the audience,
it could have been a fairy tale. Where was the
smell, I wondered. At one point in the action a
teenage boy leaves his home to go
underground and fight the Nazis – was it as
simple as that, I thought, was it? – and his
grandmother, an old, fat lady wearing a
babushka and talking with a heavy accent,
calls after him, using his Yiddish name.
Yitsalah, she calls. Yitsalah. A strange noise
began to circulate through the audience.
Yitsalah, she called. The noise grew louder.
Yitsalah, Yitsalah. Suddenly the sound was
crashing around me like a tidal wave waiting
to sweep me out to sea. Laughter. The kids
were laughing. The kids from the kibbutz
were laughing at the name, laughing at
Yitsalah, laughing at Yiddish, laughing at the
grandmother, laughing at the moon, for what
the grandmother represented might as well
have been the moon. Yitsalah, Yitsalah. The
audience repeated the name now, jabbing each
other with their elbows. My grandchildren
were laughing too. Rafi looked at me,
wondering why I wasn't joining in. I was
wearing a bright summer dress and you could
see my breasts and they were still firm and

my hair was dyed a soft brown with an
occasional blonde streak, so what could I
possibly have to do with the woman in the
babushka? With Yitsalah? I began to cry and
Rafi was no longer concerned for he thought
he saw tears of laughter.

They thought it was funny, I said to Abbie
later. So what? he replied. It's their culture, I
said. No longer, he replied, and certainly not
if they're Sephardic or African. Anyhow, we
don't speak Yiddish here, Mama, didn't you
notice? We speak Hebrew. Yiddish was
unnatural, a mutant, a mongrel; medieval
German and a bit of Russian and Turkish and
French mixed together in a blender and then
you added a little seasoning and spice,
whereas Hebrew is the language of Abraham,
Isaac and Jacob, Hebrew is our very source,
and, finally, after all these years, we have
reclaimed it. I was stunned. I actually thought
his description of Yiddish beautiful and
explained why it was so special. On the other
hand, I understood his meaning, and from his
perspective, he wasn't wrong. He was
marching into the future, wasn't he? Oh that
word – future. Every conversation about Israel
had that word in it. Still, how could I argue?
Well, I tried. It does represent something, I

said, an entire civilization, a way of life, a
way of thinking that's inspired this novel and
that symphony and a theory of relativity and a
science about the subconscious and maybe
even ideas about collective living that have in
turn inspired your kibbutz, and if it is lost
completely, if it is utterly wiped away, then
isn't that Hitler's Final Victory? That's just
meshugge, he replied. I looked at my son.
Meshugge is a Yiddish word, I said. He
laughed and walked away.

Time passed. I stopped dying my hair. The
Double Rose began to lose money; among the
many things old age isn't is profitable. Mr
Feldstein had a heart attack. I nursed him for
two years and then he passed on. I finally sat
shivah for someone who had not died before
their time – it made me feel so grown up.
Meanwhile, Miami Beach had transformed yet
again, and was suddenly – overnight – the
chic and swinging centre of America. Art
shmeco had risen from the dead, and Collins
Avenue was prime real estate. I sold Double
Rose for a fortune. The new owners liked the
name, so now Double Rose is the hottest club
in town, filled with gymnasium bodies and a
drug called Ecstasy.

I kept my apartment, it's good for them to see
an old person, I figured, and besides Rafi
likes to visit me here. Rafi and his sister Irit
left Israel some years ago. Their parents had
divorced by then. Chava remarried – a settler
on the West Bank, a man with a Bible, a beard
and a B-59. Irit moved to Rome, married a
Catholic writer, and had two children, neither
of whom are raised as Jews. Rafi moved to
Los Angeles. He's a film editor. He has – do I
have to say it – long hair and an earring, and,
in addition, a boyfriend.

A few years ago I went to visit Rafi in Los
Angeles; he showed me how he worked. Once
I understood about fast forward and jump-
cutting I realized that there was nothing
unusual about my hallucinations and that
movies were just catching up with our minds.
Rafi took me to a hill that overlooked his city,
and I told him that this abnormal metropolis
exists as it is because a dozen immigrants –
Jews from The Old Country – made their way
here seventy-five years ago and founded an
industry, what people called a dream factory,
and that in turn created our image of
American culture, it printed visions on our
minds, cossacks riding through the shtetl
became Indians attacking a wagon train, and

those images seeped into all the existing
cultures around the world, corrupting them,
enriching them, changing them for ever, and it
was all a fantasy of these little schlemiels, the
Mayers and Zukors and Warners and
Goldwyns, Goldwyn being originally
Goldfish, who had a cousin who knew my
father's sister in a little village in the Ukraine
which now lies beneath the Chernobyl dust.
Rafi's eyes glazed over; it didn't interest him.
I hugged him anyway.

That's when we went to Arizona. I wanted to
see the real West. It wasn't so real. There were
no cowboys or Indians, no stagecoaches riding
around the bend, just airless towns and
unending desert and an occasional
technicolour canyon. One day we drove for
hours in emptiness. Wherever you looked was
nothing and the scale of nothing was
awesome. Finally we reached a little souvenir
shop that stood alone in the nothing. Rafi's
car was overheating. He went inside for some
water. I walked around the front of the store.
The windows were covered with tired, touristy
watercolours of the desert. I walked inside. A
wooden Indian stood in an aisle. He held a
cigar. There was a price tag on him and above
the price the words original, not a copy. An

old man stood behind the counter, minus a
price tag. He was shouting at his son in the
stockroom. The son was middle-aged and
disturbed; desolate, I would say. The old man's
voice was too rough. I could hear a slight
accent. I looked at some more watercolours.
They were terrible. Rafi and the old man were
arguing. The old man refused to give Rafi
water. I joined Rafi at the counter. Maybe an
old lady would get some water. I noticed the
old man's hands. They were filthy and
chapped by the sun. Then I saw his arm.
There was a faded number tattooed on it. I
felt dizzy. I would never have expected that in
Arizona, in the middle of nothing. The old
man was shouting at his son again, as well as
Rafi. I wanted him to shut up. My gaze swept
up his arm to his stomach, which was gross,
and his neck, which was sagging, and then to
his face, which was like leather, and his eye,
his false eye, his false eye that looked through
me, and his other eye, the real one, the blue
one, that seemed more like a heart than an
eye, a heart that had shattered a long time
ago. We looked at each other and did not
speak. And then I turned and ran out of the
store, past the wooden Indian and the dreadful
watercolours, back into the nothing. I stared at
nothing for a long time, then returned to the
car. Rafi sat down beside me, a pail of water

on his lap. He asked me what was wrong. I
could not answer. I looked out of the car
window and saw, coming toward us, across the
prairie, a rolling tumbleweed. It blew past our
car and out again into the desert and
disappeared.

Pause.

Even though the doctor doesn't believe me
about the breathing he insists it helps to sip
water all the time. I forget to sip. I forget.

*She pours another glass of water, and drinks a
bit.*

I don't remember what I was talking about.

Pause.

Oh yes. Shivah.

Pause.

Abbie is angry at me. For sitting shivah. He
was on the phone this morning screaming at
me from Tel Aviv. He lives in Tel Aviv now
that his kibbutz has gone kaput. It's not your
business, he said. You are not one of us. And
he's right. On the other hand . . .

Sips some water.

Chava lives on the West Bank on a little
settlement that adjoins an ancient Palestinian
village. Fig trees and rock. It is, of course, in
the Bible, an ancient Hebrew village as well.
She took Doron, her youngest, with her when
she left Abbie. I went to visit several years
ago. I wanted to see my grandson, who was
still the sweetest boy, but it was odd being on
land that didn't want me, where I felt that,
ethically, I didn't belong. I remembered how
we celebrated the six-day victory in Miami
Beach and how, years later, Noam and Rutie,
drinking too much one night in the kibbutz,
told me that the spoils of war were a curse. I
didn't want to be there.

Chava did not make it easier. She kept saying
forefathers, forefathers this, forefathers that,
and then in front of my grandchild, she would

praise the memory of this man, this Baruch
someone, who massacred a group of
worshippers at the Hebron mosque. I told
Chava that was sinful. She reminded me of
the countless Jews who were themselves
massacred on this land. I know, I know, I said,
and I mourn them with a depth that even you
cannot understand, and I will mourn again
when it happens again, but that still does not
excuse this Baruch person. We're supposed to
be better than that. We're supposed to carry a
moral light unto the world. We, we, she
screamed, how can you say we, you don't
deserve to call yourself a Jew. I thought, well
– just about the time my entire family was
wiped out because they were Jewish you, my
dear, were being baptized in Kansas.

I didn't stay too long and I didn't see Doron
again until last night, when I put on the
television news and I saw his sweet, handsome
face, sweaty and strained and defiant. There
had been a riot. The settlers and the villagers.
Someone attacked someone. Someone threw a
stone. Someone was knifed. A settler fired at
the villagers. A little girl had been swept up in
the crowd. Well, maybe. Maybe she had been
throwing a stone. She was nine. A bullet
struck her in the forehead. It caught her in the

middle of a thought. Her name was Nora.
Nora el-Kareem. They interviewed the man
who fired the shot. He wasn't a man. He was
a sweet-faced boy. Doron. My blood. Son of
Yultishka. Son of the lilac tree. Child of
Warsaw. Doron. He killed a little girl. He
killed Nora el-Kareem. His grandfather sailed
a ship to a promised land. Doron. My blood.

So today I sit shivah for Nora el-Kareem. The
last of my shivahs. It is, of course, a totally
empty gesture; I know that, but I had to do
something. At first I thought I would write to
her parents and tell them I was mourning their
child, but they would hate me for patronizing
them, just as I would have hated the
grandmother of the soldier who shot Esther
had she dared to make a gesture toward me.
Esther, who I never really mourned – I was
too busy staying alive; Esther, who I never sat
shivah for on a proper wooden bench. Now
I'm sitting shivah for a little girl and it is
meaningless. A little girl who died with
Palestine on her lips. I talk to Nora in Yiddish.
It's all right, bubeleh, I say, it's all right.

Abbie is furious. Why are you doing this, he
asks. Because it's wrong. Jews don't kill little

girls. Everyone kills little girls, he shouts. It is
horrible, but every nation does it. But you are
still occupying territory, I say. Yes we are, he
replies, and although it is not nearly as
simplistic as you make it out to be, I strongly
object to it; in fact, it tears me in half and I
know that if we don't solve this soon we are
all, all of us, headed for disaster, but it is our
problem, my problem, not yours. But Israel
belongs to every Jew, I say. Only in theory, he
replies. What did you do, you bought a few
trees, you sent some money, you paid a few
visits, but did you taste it every day? It's the
difference between casual sex and a
relationship, he says, It could have been yours,
you kissed the ground before any of us, but
you chose to live as an outsider, a very
comfortable one, but an outsider nonetheless,
just as your ancestors did for centuries. So I'll
condemn my own son if I choose to, and I do
choose to, but here in my own country. I
won't let the rest of the world tell my son if
he's wrong or right. And I won't let you tell
me that Jews have to be better than everyone
else. But I'm not the rest of the world, I say,
I'm part of you. No, you're part of chopped
liver and dybbuks, he replies, that's something
different, that's the past, this is the future. I
know you hate that word, but it is our only
future. We have nothing else. Do you

understand? Everything else is gone. And then
suddenly he starts to cry. My Abbie starts to
cry. You have to let us go, Mama. Your
shadows will choke us to death. We can't
carry you with us. Your world is dead. And
then he's silent. I can tell he's embarrassed.
And then he says, You only think you're
sitting shivah for this girl. That's not what
you're sitting shivah for. What then, I ask. You
tell me, he says.

Finishes sipping the water.

There's no more water.

Turns the glass upside down.

What was I saying?

Pause.

I should get another bottle. I haven't the
energy. I hear laughter outside. Night-time in
Miami Beach. Someone is always having a
good time. Probably chemically-induced. I

don't belong here, Abbie is right. But there
was always a joy in not belonging. Did I
belong in Yultishka? Or Warsaw? Or
anywhere? Restless minds . . . what did I say?
. . . a restless people produce restless minds.

Pause.

Maybe God is just a question like everything
else.

Pause.

I'm thirsty, The truth is wooden benches are
very uncomfortable. But I have to mourn a
little girl, don't I? It's all right, bubeleh, it's
all right. Sleep my child, sleep. Sweet Nora.
My Esther. Shall I sing you a song? Of
course, that's the other thing about sitting
shivah, you can sing songs. How about a song
from a movie? A movie I saw in Warsaw on
Krochmalna Street. With Yussel. We had just
been to a café. I think there was some kind of
fight. Over poetry. How stupid. No, maybe
someone owed someone else money. Or had
slept with someone's friend. I don't remember.
Anyhow, in the movie, Molly Picon was

making a fool of herself. It took place in a
shtetl, but it was a shtetl made of cardboard. It
was a set. Or maybe it was Yultishka. Yussel
put his hand under my blouse while she sang.

Sings.

> 'Yiddle mit a fiddle . . .
> Yiddle, Yiddle, Yiddle . . .'

Stops.

And his hand pinched my breast . . .

Pause.

What was I saying?

Pause.

Sings.

'Yiddle, Yiddle, Yiddle . . .'

Pause.

I think that song is a silly thing to remember.
On the other hand . . .

She gasps.

She suddenly cannot catch her breath.

She closes her eyes . . .